the
words
i'll
never
say

alana kirby

THE OUTSIDER **POET** PRESS

trigger warning

some of these poems contain topics related to:

homophobia

sexism

racism

abuse

bullying

sexual assault

eating disorders

suicide

the

    words

  i'll

    never

      say

the

moments

that

broke

me

the

most

i fell in love with you. at least i think
i did. there used to be no doubt in my
mind that my feelings for you were
true.

you used to make me smile every
time you called me on the phone and
you used to be the reason i looked
forward to each day.

my love for you was beyond galaxies
and i saw the rest of my forever in your
eyes.

i thought i knew you.

but these days, i find it impossible to
get even an ounce of love out of you.
you stare right through me as though
i've never meant a damn thing and
suddenly i'm not what you want.

so now i lay awake at night asking
myself the same tiring question. ***"am
i in love with you, or am i in love with a
version of you that no longer exists?"***

i didn't quite understand at first why
you were so special to me.
i didn't understand why you stood out
from the rest.
everything about you was magical.
a type of love i couldn't feel for
anybody else.
even on our worst days, i would've
never left your side.
you know i didn't want things to
change.
but i missed you so much it hurt.
i couldn't sleep most nights and my
pillow was stained with tears.
even hearing your name filled me with
pain.
i would've given anything to turn
back the clocks, to be with you one last
time.
i never told you how much your
absence tore me apart, even if i know
i should have.
i'm sorry i let you down as much as
i did.
i hope you know i still love you the
same.

i realized it was over as we stood there
in a painful silence.
this was the end of our story.
i wanted to burst into tears and beg you
to stay.
it wouldn't have changed a thing.

there was once a point in time when
i wanted to spend the rest of my life
having fun with you and making
memories we'd never be able to forget.
that was back when we were too young
to understand how difficult things can
get.

people change as they grow, right?
this world will break even the most
resilient and losing you showed me how
fast everything can change.

**you had abandoned me long before
i met you.**

it took me a long time to realize that
i would never get over you. i'll admit
that i'm completely terrified of how
much i want you. i think of you every
passing minute that i'm awake. i never
understood the reason why you
looked at me with such love in your
eyes. i never understood what you saw
in someone like me.
i know i didn't deserve you. i didn't
deserve to feel your kiss or the touch of
your hands slowly becoming entangled
with mine. i didn't deserve the
wonderful late night calls or to hear the
words *"i love you"* fall from your
precious lips. you saved my life with
nothing more than the comfort of being
lost in your presence. ***darling, loving
you is the only thing in my life i've ever
done right.***

i really did adore you. i desperately
wanted to be the person who made you
feel as though you'd stumbled upon the
gift of your soul being at home. i fell in
love with the idea of your potential
and i fell apart when the illusions began
to fade into nothingness. i thought
i knew you. i thought i'd memorized
every crevice and secret kept within
your soul. it tore me apart to realize
that i had never truly met you. i grew
attached to a version of you that didn't
exist. every laugh we shared, every
smile we exchanged meant nothing to
you. i saw the best despite having the
worst of intentions. i foolishly adored
the false light you had created. in the
end, it didn't matter what i saw or what
i hopelessly believed you felt. you never
loved me. *and i only loved the person
i wanted to believe you were.*

i've spent my entire life feeling alone.

i liked the silence at first.

it kept me convinced i was in control
even though it broke my heart.

i was afraid to love you.

i was afraid to admit i'd found
someone who gave me more than
loneliness ever could.

i adored you more than anyone else.

you made me want to stop hiding from
the world.

so i know that i needed you.

you were the first person i ever did.

i know it's time for me to let you go.

i won't forget the precious memories or the way that i loved you. i won't forget your smile or your comforting laugh. my heart will always cherish the beauty of the love we once had.

we used to dream of our future together. we used to promise that we'd spend the rest of our lives falling in love with one another.

and i meant every word that i spoke to you. you truly did mean the world to me. i hope you know that you still do.

so i will continue to remember you even though you're gone.

i will continue to love you even though i'm making the choice to let go of you.

i imagined a future where i could be
with you. i dreamed of our wedding day
and how the words "*i do*" would fall
from your lips.

i dreamed of early mornings filled with
the smell of coffee and the sound of our
children laughing.

that sounds simple, doesn't it? you
were special enough to make a life
like that seem worth living.

i wish you had stayed. i think about the
way things would be if you did.

and so i dreamed of a future where
i could be with you. ***i dreamed of a
future that we'll never get the chance
to live.***

i adored her.
from the way her long hair fell just
above her waist to her gorgeous laugh.
she was nothing short of an angel.
i needed her.
from the way she kissed me to the
comfort that came with being wrapped
up in her arms.
she lit up every room.

we were only best friends, right?
nothing more, nothing less.
we were two girls who had found their
sense of home in one another.
maybe we dressed the same, did our
hair and makeup the same.
and i was too afraid to tell you the
truth.
**best friends don't look at each other
the way i looked at you.**

i remember the day i fell in love with
you. it was in that moment that
i realized i'd never be the same. i never
understood why you looked at me like
i was somehow worth more than the
world. you made me feel like i was
finally enough.

i know that this is my fault. if i could go
back and change things, i promise you
i would. but i know it doesn't matter.
you're never coming back. even if i can't
understand why, even if i'm the reason
for your absence, *i'll love you until the
stars stop shining and the sun no
longer rises in the sky.*

we were young and dumb when we fell
in love.
reality hadn't yet set in and our
fantasies were easier to live in.
we dreamed of our future together as if
we stood a chance at having one.
i couldn't have imagined a life without
you.

i still miss what we had.
i miss when things were easier.
it breaks my heart to have let us down.
i'm sorry i couldn't be who you needed
me to.
i hope you know that i still love you.

i adore the lines that form under your
eyes when you smile and the way you
could touch me without using your
hands. you're all of my blessings and
each of my curses. but i can never tell if
the highs are worth the pain.

your touch is a poison that lingers on
my skin and you've become an
addiction i know i won't beat. if only
i was worth enough to make you stay.
but while i was busy seeing the universe
in your eyes, **you could only bring
yourself to see the stars in mine.**

people ask me why i stay with you.
i know it doesn't make much sense.
most days you treat me like i'm nothing
and you make me feel completely
alone. i wish i understood why some
part of me refuses to let you go.

there are days where you want me
more than anything else. there are days
where your love is enough to make me
feel whole. you hold me in your arms
like you'll never let me go. *and for the
first time in my life, i don't feel alone.*

everyone knew how much i adored
you.
how could they have not?
your love gave me so much strength.
my world became whole at nothing
more than the touch of your fingertips.
all of my fear would fall away when you
whispered my name.
**and suddenly none of my monsters
brought me any pain.**

you're not the same. the you i fell in
love with no longer exists.
i miss the way things used to be. i miss
calling on the phone and laughing until
we couldn't breathe. you held the key
to my heart. that's why i hated seeing
you change.

i couldn't stop it though.
i was forced to watch you turn into
someone i didn't know.

i live through our memories for
comfort. i miss the sound of your voice
and the feeling of your hands in mine.
i'll never get that back. *i miss the
version of you i used to have.*

our relationship was never good. it was one that was constantly filled with pain. for a long time, i thought it was my fault. i couldn't help but justify you. even when you'd go days without speaking to me or would force me to shut out everyone but you. no matter what, it was never enough to make you happy.

i didn't want to admit that you were hurting me. maybe i was afraid of the truth.

i desperately clung onto the good moments so that i could keep this image of you. **and i looked past the bad for fear of what you'd turn into.**

"do you still care about me?" i asked as salty tears dripped down my cheeks. your expression was cold. i could feel your eyes piercing through mine and your face was completely still. you sat there silent as the seconds that passed grew deafening. i wanted to scream until my lungs were burning like hell. *"no, i don't anymore"* you replied without any visible remorse. i couldn't hold it in anymore. my gentle tears turned into a riptide of sobs that drowned out all of my senses.

but that was years ago. i've learned to be just like you, burying my bitter emotions under denial. and if you were to ask me that same question i had asked you all those years ago, *"do you still care about me?"* i would stare back at you with a mask too strong to read past; my eyes devoid of any and all emotion. *"no, i don't anymore"* **i've become a liar like you.**

there are days where i still think about
you. if i'm being honest, it's most days
that i do. i thought i would've let you go
by now. but the truth is that i don't
know how to.

the sound of your laughter haunts me.
the thought of never hearing it again
hurts my soul. your smile is still the
most beautiful one i've ever seen and
i wish i knew how to stop myself
from loving you. it's so hard to imagine
going on without you. ***it's even harder
because i know i have to.***

maybe i was misunderstood. you
always looked at me like i was a puzzle
you couldn't piece together. you spent
so long trying to figure out what was
wrong with me. you didn't see the pain
i was in. you looked past the cries for
help and the loneliness i felt.

i was lost for a long time. i couldn't
remember who i was. it felt like i was
drowning, thrashing around and
begging for you to save me.
i was thousands of feet underwater.
**but you never noticed that i couldn't
breathe.**

you tell yourself you don't miss them. but what would you do if they were standing in front of you again? how would you feel and what would you say? would you truly be at peace with everything that's happened?

you can try to ignore that lingering feeling of grief. the truth is that you might even succeed. you can try to drown out the pain of knowing you'll never hear their laugh again and you can try to forget all of the precious things they said. ***but you don't realize how much you miss someone until they're standing in front of you again.***

i still think of you every day.
i think of your smile and i think of your
laugh.
i think of how i loved you more than
anyone else.
i truly hoped the pain of losing you
would go away by now.
but even as the seasons change and
time goes by, our memories are the
only thing that lingers in my mind.
so darling, what do i do if i never stop
loving you?
what do i do if i never let you go?

my mind is plagued with memories of
you.
they follow me from the moment
i wake up to the moment i fall asleep.
there's never a moment where i don't
think of you.
i wonder if my absence hurts you the
way it hurts me.
deep down, i'm scared that you've
moved on.
but it broke my heart to watch you
leave.
***so now i sit here waiting for the
day you'll come back to me.***

i can feel your absence slowly killing
me.
it hurts like nothing ever has before.
i wish i could see your face.
i wish i could hold you and tell you how
much i miss you.
i wonder if you feel as lost as i do.
i know it's selfish that i want you to.

i texted you the other day to ask you if
you still missed me.
deep down, i already knew what you'd
say.
maybe i secretly hoped for a different
answer anyway.

you're still my everything, you know?
it's no wonder i had faith.

you told me you didn't miss me
anymore.
you told me you'd already moved on.
***and the reason that hurts so much is
because i never knew how to.***

of course, this is just another poem
i'm writing about someone who could
never love me as much as i love them.

maybe that's my biggest flaw.
i feel too much. that's why it became
easy for me to shut everything off.
it saved me the pain of living with my
heart. i've spent my life wondering why
love has failed me so many times.
wondering if it was my fault for not
being someone else. i wanted so bad
for you to be my answer. i wanted you
to be the reason i finally understood
why.

but perhaps sometimes it's the
greatest questions that don't have an
answer.

i hope you know you're the reason for
my broken heart.
i hope you know that although i smile
and say it doesn't hurt me,
***the truth is i'm afraid i'll never let go of
you.***

my mind can't help but wander when
i see you. i try to stop myself but
i'm never able to.

i can't help but imagine what it would
be like to hold you. to touch you and
tell you how wonderful you are.

it's amazing how you do it all so
effortlessly. you take my breath away
without even trying. i hate that
i'm forced to love you from afar.

and what we have isn't real. darling,
i know it never will be. *but i still
imagine a world where you're mine
anyway.*

i'm too afraid to tell people the truth.
i'm too afraid to tell people about the
way she makes me feel alive or how
much i adore her. i know they wouldn't
understand.

i hope someday i'll have the privilege of
hearing you say the words "*i do*".
it just hurts because my heart didn't fall
in love with a man. ***it fell in love with
you.***

i know you think of me when you're
with him. i know he doesn't know about
the countless nights you've spent in my
room with nothing but our clothes on
the floor or the way you kiss me like
i'm worth more than the world.

darling, i know you'll never tell him and
i know he'll never figure it out. i know
you'll never admit to loving me. i know
you're terrified of the idea.

and so, you call me a friend because
that's all two girls could ever be. **but
you touch me when we're alone
because it's different when no one can
see.**

you only ever came back because you
knew how much i needed you. and you
always said i was wrong for so foolishly
believing you needed me too. but tell
me, why couldn't you bring yourself to
let me go? why did my absence tear you
apart? if i truly didn't mean a thing,
then why did you miss me like i did?
i realize now that you were afraid. you
were constantly torn between the
choice of loving me or letting go
because your heart had been broken so
many times before. and the truth is that
you looked at me like i was one in a
million. you looked at me like i was
different. like i was the only person
who'd ever made you feel understood.
so to me, it was okay. *because i wanted
you to love me more than i wanted to
admit you never could.*

there are days where i'm left convinced
i'm over you. there are days where
i wake up with a smile on my face
even though you're no longer laying
next to me. i'm proud of myself for
letting you go. i don't need you in order
to feel okay. i don't need you for
anything at all. i was wrong to have
convinced myself you meant so much.

there are days where i can't get you out
of my head. there are nights where
i'm up until 4AM because our memories
won't leave me alone. i can't imagine
spending the rest of my life without
you. *i was wrong to have convinced
myself i could let you go.*

it was as though you took every piece of
me with you when you left. and with it,
you took everything that used to make
the world whole. it's almost as funny as
it is sad to think about how much
i loved you.
you never loved me back.
if you had, things would've been
different.

but you felt as empty inside as i do now.
you blamed me for every single one of
your mistakes and you took and you
took until i had nothing left to give. *so
even after all these years, i don't
understand the reason i turned into
you despite everything you did.*

loving you was the first time in my life
i truly felt alive. you see, i was always
lost. broken and in pain. i never
understood the privilege of being loved.
but my world changed when i met you.
you opened up my eyes to the
possibility of finally being enough. you
set my soul on fire in a way i'd never
known before and you held me like
i was worth everything.
maybe i should've realized it was too
good to be true. i got so lost in this
feeling of finally holding the gift of love
inside my hands that i didn't realize it
wasn't enough.
i know now it hurts less to walk through
life only ever knowing pain. *i know now
it hurts more to find that love and be
forced to watch it slip away.*

i'd always told myself that i was cursed
to be alone. and no matter how much
i tried to change this, it was always true.
my heart was full of madness and my
head of fear. perhaps the reason i was
so in love with chaos was because i held
so much of it within me. but i was afraid
of who i was. and for that, i lived life
from my head, never from my heart.

i'd spent a lifetime trying to find
comfort in the way my loneliness held
onto me. after all, it was the only thing
i'd ever known. but you reminded me of
the beauty that comes from madness.
you took a girl who was nothing and
made her seem beautiful. the way you
wrapped your arms around me made
me feel like i could finally breathe.
***and you were the first and only
person to ever fall in love with me.***

this

time

i'll

leave

a

light

on

alana kirby

people told me i'd never survive
because my insight would hold me
down.
tell me, what's so weak about
understanding the deepest parts of
yourself?
if anything, it takes true bravery to stare
into your own darkness time and time
again and still stand tall.
i see that i'm powerful because i don't
fear the idea of getting to know even
the most miserable parts of myself.
i see that i'm strong because i've felt
enough to send me crashing,
yet i carry on.

i really do hate myself.
i hate the way my hair falls beside my
face and the way my eyes glisten in the
sun.
i hate waking up and looking in the
mirror to see my least favorite person
staring back.
from the way my chest rises and
falls when i breathe to the buried
emotions i've been too lost to confront,
i can't stand any part of me.

i really am afraid of myself.
i'm afraid the words i speak are not the
truth and that i've forgotten who i am.
i'm afraid nothing will ever be enough
to make me feel whole. from the way
i can barely contain my shame to the
nightmares that come alive in my head
every night, *i wish i had the courage to
accept myself.*

i feel sorry for my younger self. i feel
sorry for the version of me that was
chasing after the approval of others
in order to feel complete.

it hurts when you can no longer
remember who you are and your
identity is a lie created to comfort the
hole inside of your heart.

her smile is made up of so much
strength. she has lived through hell but
still has the courage to believe in better
days. she has seen the darkness that
covers the world but still adores those
precious moments that remind her how
much good exists behind the hurt.

she doesn't see how capable she is. she
doesn't realize how much beauty
her light can build. *i wish i could tell her
how wonderful she is.*

i'm afraid that i've forgotten who
i truly am. the girl in the mirror feels
like a stranger i can only vaguely
remember. we share the same mouth,
eyes and hands. we have loved the
same people, though in different ways.

she's the voice in my head that's
begging so hard to be released. after all
of these years, i can still hear her
dark, lonely and pained screams. she
cries out during the night, *"why am
i still not worthy of loving me?"*

i can see it in her eyes. the longing to be
no one but herself. i've grown tired of
the masks and the empty games of
charades. i want her to come home.
i miss every hurting part of her
beautiful soul.
so let me love you back to life. let me
give you everything the world couldn't.
**it doesn't make you broken to be
different from the mold.**

at the end of the day, she finds herself alone. it's not a physical loneliness. it's not something that can be fixed by the touch of a lover's hand or a false life made up of people that adore her. it's the pain of knowing that nobody sees her. after all, how can anybody notice her if she isn't truly there?

she parades around in a mask created by those who told her she wasn't good enough. she abandoned herself for a society that doesn't understand how to accept her. she's alone because she doesn't have anyone. ***she's alone because she doesn't even have herself.***

i sit on the bathroom floor with my
hands covering my face.
a couple hundred calories wasn't that
much to swallow. a couple hundred
quickly turned into thousands.
i don't remember the point at which
i gave up control. all i can recall is an
empty feeling created by this body that
i'm forced to live in.

i eat with a broken hope that i'll end up
forgetting my pain.
it's a temporary relief. i know that
i'll regret it each time i give into it again.
but it's in those moments that i finally
feel free. it's in those moments that
i'm able to forget every lonely feeling
buried deep within me.

food became my only friend and my
only escape. ***nobody understands the
darkness this type of comfort brings.***

we're taught to hide from ourselves
because it's seen as weak to confront
the feelings we get told are meant to
stay locked away.
we learn to ignore ourselves through
listening to others.
our identities are made up of the
opinions formed by those who don't
truly know us.

and it's true that words aren't enough
to break our bones or cause us to bleed.
**but to heal a broken bone is easier
than to heal a broken soul.**

she was a girl who wasn't loved right.
nothing hurt her worse than having to
live with that.
it destroyed her to exist this way
because it wasn't who she is.
she used to have a heart full of love.
she used to be so desperate to give
others the happiness that she couldn't
give herself.
even as things got better, even as she
started to notice the good in the
world, her fear didn't go away.
people tried to reach her heart. people
tried to show her that she was more
than where she'd been.
but she was too afraid of what would
happen if she were to let someone in.

if you look hard enough, you can see
the light that envelopes the world**.**
maybe things aren't as hopeless as they
seem. maybe there's broken pieces of
beauty in everything.

i know you think things are hopeless.
someday things will find a way to mend.
there's light in knowing that even if
your world is made up of darkness, ***the
sun will somehow rise again.***

i want you to know you're beautiful.
yes you, the person reading this.
your beauty goes beyond what other
people can see.
i know it's unfair.
i understand how lonely it feels.
the absence of their acceptance doesn't
change how wonderful you are.
maybe society labels you as broken or
tells you to change.
it doesn't mean a thing.
you have the most precious soul.
**you're worth more than they'll ever
know.**

i'm a girl who's spent her life feeling
misunderstood. it's made me afraid of
the world.

maybe the problem is that i don't
blindly pretend to be someone i'm not.
i don't try to change the girl in the
mirror. i understand i deserve more
than that.

i've been told time and time again that
being different is a sin.
it's always from the mouths of people
who are afraid of those who aren't the
same as them.
but i don't care what people think.
i don't even care if no one listens to
what i have to say.
**i'm brave enough to stand apart in a
society full of people who are too
afraid to change.**

i remember the year i tried to kill
myself. i remember the exact day, time,
and place. but most of all, i remember
how hopeless i felt.
isn't it sad how broken someone must
be to do such a thing?
it's the feeling as though everything's
dark. that there's not a single light to
be found. it's that empty feeling of
waking up every day and just
immediately wanting to go back to bed.
when you're just so tired of your pain
that you become convinced there's no
other choice. it's not even the feeling of
wanting to die. ***it's the feeling of giving
up because you've tried so hard and
you still don't understand how it feels
to be alive.***

eight things most people don't know about me

one. i have a really big heart

two. for as long as i can remember, i've always felt alone

three. i don't tell most people how i feel

four. if i've told you how i feel, you probably mean a lot to me

five. i used to be afraid of the dark. but i find comfort in it now

six. i often find myself having trouble seeing any good in the world

seven. most of the people in my life have hurt me

*eight. **i wish i knew how to love myself without the approval of others***

i've felt empty for years.
it's like this inexplicable feeling that
something is missing and i don't know
how to replace it.
sometimes i miss the simple things, like
laughing with friends or happily dancing
around my room. somehow nothing
lights me up anymore.
i miss those little things.
i miss being okay.

you're beautiful.
i'll keep on repeating those words until
you believe it.
because i want you to know there's
nothing wrong with you.
because i want you to love yourself for
all of the things that society has taught
you not to.

we're taught from a young age that
our bodies don't belong to us.
men will touch and grab, not listening
when we beg for them to stop.

you're a prude if you refuse to give
yourself away and a slut once you do.
the beauty of what exists inside our
hearts is not worth what the curves that
roam our bodies are.
despite our constant pleading to be
seen as more than what we are, our
voices still go unheard.

yet we're worth more than the hands of
a million men and capable of more than
they'll ever know. ***to exist in this world
as a woman is a strength in and of
itself.***

the truth is that i'm angry.
i always have been.
people ask me why as if it doesn't
make sense.
i can't forget the darkness i've seen.
i can't ignore the emptiness in me.
i've tried and i've tried but things
never seem to change.

the truth is that i'm in pain.
tell me, how could i not be?
it's as though things will never get
better and i don't know what to do.
it's as though my brokenness won't let
go of me.
**it's as though part of me
doesn't even want it to.**

i find our society heartbreaking.
i find it heartbreaking that little girls
start shaving at the age of 9 because
they're told it makes them more
desirable.
i find it heartbreaking that we'll take
away someone's right to live based off
the color of their skin.
i find it heartbreaking that we're told
we aren't beautiful unless we look a
certain way.
i find it heartbreaking that women can't
walk alone at night for the fear of being
raped.
i find it heartbreaking that there
are people who view life as something
so hopeless that they can't find a
reason to keep going.
and i find it heartbreaking that we just
accept this.
i find it heartbreaking that we accept
this broken, empty society as
something whole.

i can feel my loneliness surrounding
me. that's the problem. it always has
been. i feel so painfully empty inside.
it's as if something that's meant to be
there is missing.

i don't know myself anymore. i can't
remember who i am or who i used to
be. i can't remember what lights me up
inside or what puts a smile on my face.
all i know is that there's an emptiness
inside me that i can't seem to fill.

i can no longer recognize the girl in the
mirror. she's become a stranger.
i keep on asking her who she is. **but she
never answers back.**

i don't have an eating disorder. this is
something i'm certain of. even when
i replace meals with coffee or spend
hours a day obsessing over the scale,
i tell myself i'm fine.
even though it's the only thing that
makes me feel in control and the only
friend i can turn to, i tell myself it's
normal.

this isn't a sickness or a sign that i'm in
pain. this isn't proof that i'm not okay.
and despite the fact that i can't stand
who i see in the mirror, that i'm killing
myself just to make her thinner.
i don't have an eating disorder. **this is
something i'm certain of.**

someday you'll stumble upon the love
that you deserve.
someday all of the sleepless nights and
troubles weighing you down will be
worth it.
i know you're tired of breathing.
that you want to give in to the
emptiness inside of your soul.
how do you fight when living feels like a
chore that you don't have the energy to
do anymore?

there will come a day when the hurt
begins to fall away.
who you are goes beyond the shadows
that haunt your heart.
even when you can barely force
yourself out of bed and your world feels
as though it's falling apart, i want you to
stay.
even though it can be so hard to
find, *i know that someday you'll
understand how it feels to be alive.*

you'll never be whole until you find
peace with yourself.
i think that's what most people fail to
realize.
you could have everything you've ever
wanted.
you could hold the world in your hands.
even then, it'd never be enough.
you would still feel incomplete.
you can try to ignore it.
you can try to push it down.
**but you'll always feel like something's
missing if you don't have yourself.**

i was born with a heart that feels
everything.
whether it's the touch of rain on my
skin or the sound of birds singing in the
morning.
i can find meaning in anything.
the world doesn't appreciate people
like me.
it thoughtlessly labels me broken and
tells me to change.
i won't mask myself and play a part.
it doesn't mean i'm broken.
**it means the world should change its
heart.**

she was never conventionally beautiful. she had a way about her that looks alone couldn't define. you could see the buried pain in her eyes and all of the thoughts that kept her up at night. there was a longing inside her to feel whole. truth be told, she never recognized her own light. she wasn't conventionally beautiful. but she could make even the darkest of days seem bright. she had a way about her that made you feel alive. that darling, that was what made her stand out from the rest. ***that was what made her so beautiful.***

i realized i was growing up when there
came a day i stopped coming outside
to play with my friends.
i stopped laughing and i stopped going
to birthday parties.
i took off the glasses and i stopped
seeing the world from my rose colored
view.
i think life has never been what
i thought i knew to be true.

i think the reason so many of us fall in
love with the memories from our
childhood is because it felt easier to
venture through life with that innocent
spark. we were too young to
understand most things.
maybe to some it's beautiful to live life
with the fear of confronting the
unknown. but i like to think it's
beautiful to wander through the
darkness and still come out on the
other side saying *"life truly is
something worth living."*

finally starting to love yourself is the
scariest feeling in the world.
you realize so much about yourself that
you didn't before.
you finally understand the reasons why
you behaved the way you did and why
you loved the people you did.
everything you thought you knew
about yourself turns out to be an
illusion.

it took finding this little bit of love for
myself to realize that everything i was
doing was an attempt to fill the space
inside me. the space where i was
supposed to be.
*it took finding this little bit of love for
myself to accept that the people i once
loved were nothing but replacements
for the love i couldn't give to myself.*

i hope the world treats you better than
it treated me.
i hope you wake each morning feeling
lighter than the one before and i hope
you're never put in a position where
you have to question your worth.
i hope the words of others don't break
your soul and i hope you can always
find a reason to believe.
because you deserve it.
**you deserve so much better than what
the world gave to me.**

the hardest lesson i've had to learn is
that things always have the potential
to get better. hope comes from some of
the most mysterious places. whether
it's from the kindness of a stranger or
the touch of a lover. things are never as
lonely as they seem.

the truth is that someone out there
cares. and although i may not know you
or the pain that you're going through,
i love you entirely.

so i will do everything to help you
remember you aren't alone. i will pour
my heart into poetry and into words.
because i want you to know that
somehow things have to get better.

i've carried the weight of the world on
my shoulders since i was a little girl.
*i've watched everything i love die in
front of me and gotten back up as
though it didn't ruin me.*

i won't allow my voice to be a whisper
anymore. i won't allow it to be ignored
or to go unheard. the world will hear
me shout. ***even if it's through nothing
but pages full of words.***

she wanted to be seen.
not looked at.
not dressed up to be someone she
wasn't.
she wanted to be accepted for who she
was.

she wanted her light to be seen as
bright and beautiful, rather than harsh
and blinding.
she wanted to be taught to love who
she was, **rather than taught how to
hide it.**

she sits alone inside an empty room,
cradling herself back and forth.
the terrifying thing is that she's been
here for years, trapped inside this room
with no real form of comfort.
just crying and screaming at these
lifeless walls, begging them *"please let
me go."*

i wonder how she would feel if there
was someone around to tell her that
she's the reason for her pain,
if there was someone around to tell her
that she's the one who shut herself in.

it's true that the door is locked.
the only thing she doesn't see is that
it's locked from the inside.
**and she has more power than she's
ever allowed herself to realize.**

i never understood why i wasn't
enough. even now, i still struggle to
comprehend. i know the world has
never been right or fair. that didn't
mean i deserved it. i didn't deserve the
burden of having to walk through life
feeling alone. i didn't deserve the nights
i spent crying on my bedroom floor,
desperately trying to understand why
i wasn't deserving of the same kind of
love. because i watched the world
around me find comfort in one another.
i watched them receive the acceptance
i didn't. and sure, it was the words of
others that broke my heart. ***but it was
the pain of knowing i'd never be
enough that broke my soul.***

i want you to know it gets better than
this. i want you to know you're worth
every star in the sky.
because even though you can't see a
star next to the blinding light of the
sun, that doesn't mean it isn't there.
even if you've always felt painfully
invisible, even if the world broke your
heart or left you scarred, that didn't
mean it was your fault.
stars shine for a different reason.
they guide us when we're lost. they
light up our skies when we're
surrounded by nothing but miles of pain
and darkness. and they remind us that
sometimes it's the lights that go
unnoticed, the ones that shine while
the world isn't awake to see them.
**sometimes those are the lights we
need the most.**

i've been giving my entire life in hopes of receiving a love that i'm not entirely sure exists anymore. people tell me it's all in my head. that i'll magically wake up someday and feel at peace with the world despite all the ways in which it's broken me. that i'll someday crawl my way out of the darkness and learn to see again.

yet i'm completely beaten down and exhausted. i've run out of reasons to believe. ***and i'm just so tired of fighting when no one's ever fought for me.***

i wish i didn't care so much. that's all i've ever wanted. to venture through life without fearing the unknown. to stop obsessing over every little flaw, every little detail. to finally feel alive. but it's like i'm being restrained, held back, but it isn't by anyone but me. it's like i'm watching my life pass me by, ***waiting for the day where i'll finally wake up and set myself free.***

the

secrets

of

my

heart

i was a girl who fell in love with another
girl.
i fell in love with the way she did
her hair, the color of her eyes, her
gorgeous sense of style.
i fell in love with making her laugh, the
way she made me feel alive, her perfect
smile.
i guess i was wrong. at least that's what
people told me.
i secretly grew bitter over the cruel
words and disapproving stares of
others.
i found comfort through the feeling of
my hand intertwined with hers.
i felt at home with the touch of her lips.

i think people fear what they can't bring
themselves to understand. but i'm tired
of denying what i feel.
i don't want a man to hold me close.
i don't ever want to be with one.
so what if i feel this way?
**it's not like i have the choice to
change.**

i left a photo of us hanging on my
bedroom wall. you had a look of pure
joy painted inside of your eyes.
i remember the late summer nights we
spent running around beneath a
moonlit sky and the way we laughed as
though we felt alive.

you'll forever be my muse until the day
that i die. i'll love you until the sun no
longer adorns the sky and the world
stops spinning.

this life truly is something worth living.
you're my favorite reason why.

someday we'll dance around our
kitchen with nothing but the
streetlights pouring in from the open
windows to illuminate our shadows. my
arms wrapped around you will be
enough to keep us safe. even as we
grow old, we won't lose that spark that
keeps us desperate to explore every
part of this world.
you're my feeling of home.
i don't care if people call us fools
or say we're too young to know what
forever means.
this won't fade with age. i won't grow
tired of kissing your lips, but instead
i will grow to miss them each time
they're not there.
you're a gift.
i know there is nobody in this world
quite like you. i promise to spend the
rest of my life, ***the rest of our life falling
in love with you.***

with your fingers tracing down my
spine and a smile forming on your face,
you somehow never fail to take my
breath away. you're the most precious
soul i've ever known. as i'm lying on
your chest, you leave me with a feeling
that everything's okay. fear no longer
hurts my heart. you say that
i'm enough. you effortlessly fill me up
with strength. you're the galaxies that
exist behind my eyelids. you're the stars
that wander throughout the night,
reminding me how wonderful it feels to
dream. i will love you until my dying
breath. ***darling, you're everything to
me.***

i don't care what people say. i don't
care if i'm labeled as a sin or if nobody
accepts what i feel. she sets my heart
on fire in a way that a man never could.
i'm not wrong for wanting her instead
of him. a love this pure couldn't be
wrong. i find comfort simply through
the gentle sound of her voice. she's
such an angel. from the way her eyes
light up when she smiles to the feeling
of being wrapped up in her arms,
i know she's the one for me.
and they tell me it's so frightening that
i could be a girl who's fallen for another
girl. none of that matters to me.
let them all stare.
let them see how much i love you.

you have the most beautiful smile.
it's the only one that can take my
breath away. the way the corners of
your mouth crease when you laugh.
the way your eyes light up with joy.
you make everything feel magical.
your happiness is worth more than my
weight in gold.
i really do adore you. i want to give you
all that i can, to show you how lovely
you are. no one else compares to you.
nobody matters like you do.

she feels like a dream. her smile fills me with hope and her laugh brings me bliss. my soul aches for hers. i want to keep her safe from the darkness that covers the world. my arms will be a blanket of comfort for when she's hurt. i'll make sure that she's never left feeling alone. there's something magical about the way she makes me feel. her mind is filled with millions of wonders that i have yet to explore. ***her heart holds all of the answers that i've spent my life searching for.***

i was lost before i met you. i'd become convinced i was completely alone. it seemed like there was nothing i could do. my world had crashed and burned before my eyes and i didn't understand why.

you looked at me like i was beautiful despite my pain. you helped me find the strength i didn't know i had. you're my angel on earth. i love you for all that you've done. ***you gave me the gift of hope when i was certain that i had none.***

you have the most beautiful soul. the hands of the universe carefully crafted you from stardust.

you're my feeling of comfort. you remind me of heaven and feel like home. there's no one else i'd rather have. i'll love you through our darkest days and hold you until the sun rises. **my love, i'll never let you go.**

i secretly imagined a future with you.
we'd slow dance around an empty
room at four in the morning with a
smile clinging to our faces. life would
never grow to be boring as long as i was
with you.
you'd make me laugh on days when
i couldn't remember how to smile.
i'd fall asleep in your arms every
night because they'd remind me of how
it feels to be safe.
and there was no one that could
replace you.
you have the most wonderful heart i've
ever known.
**you're worth everything to me and
more.**

i'm in love with everything about her

i'm in love with the freckles that kiss
her face.
the smile she wears despite all of her
pain.
the parts of her she doesn't allow
anyone else to see.
the courage she gives me to believe.

i'm in love with the sound of her
laughter.
the color of her eyes.
the pain she tries so hard to hide.
and the hope she's somehow still able
to find.

i'm in love with her.

our love isn't like those romance
movies. it's rather simple, yet still
perfectly sweet. i don't need someone
to bring flowers onto my doorstep.
i don't need fancy wine mixed with
expensive dinners or to wake up to long
good morning texts everyday. i mean,
why would i? i believe your presence is
worth more than every luxury in this
world. you bring me contentment
simply through existing. you take the
worst of days and turn them into
something good with nothing more
than the touch of your hands.
i'm able to believe that happiness exists
because i have the gift of being able to
spend this life with you. i don't need
any of those lavish things. ***you're more
than enough for my heart.***

i need you in my life. what would i do
without the soft sound of your voice
and the reminders that i'm still enough?
who would i be without your touch?
nobody makes me feel the way you do.
nothing is worth more than your love.
you know i'd be lost without you.

you see me. you always have. most
people look at me and notice nothing
more than the broken shell of a girl.
it's the reason why i've always felt
alone.

you're different.
i feel understood when i'm with you.
you love me for who i am. you love me
for every fault and perfection. you love
me for my soul.

you've stared into my darkness and
somehow managed to find a light.
you've found beauty in the parts of me
that no one else could.
you don't see a broken person or a
mess that can't be fixed. you see the
real me. ***that's why i love you.***

i barely knew you. i barely knew the sound of your voice or the comfort of your touch. *but i fell in love.* it's not one of those things that words can explain. you just felt different from the rest of the world. you had this spark about you that no one else did. something that precious can't be ignored. *so i fell in love with you. i fell in love* with the light you gave to me. **and i fell in love with the way you made me believe.**

i used to be afraid of love. it seemed
like the only option at the time. my
heart had been bruised and broken.
i couldn't find a reason to believe.

i thank the universe every day for pulling
you into my life. there was once a time
when the thought of love left me
feeling defeated. ***but darling, you're
the courage i never knew i needed.***

you're beautiful.
words can't explain how much so.
there's something about you that's out
of this world.
every inch of my soul lights up when
you whisper my name and i can't
help but adore the smile that touches
your face.

i hope you always remember how much
i love you.
i hope the reminders shower you with
hope and let you know that you're
enough.
because the truth is that you are.
you're so infinitely enough.

my world changed when i met you. you looked at me like i was more than what i was and you made me feel like i was finally enough. you're the light that guides me when i'm lost. ***your love has given me more than i could've ever thought.***

there's something so beautiful about
you. something that no one else has.
maybe it's the way you make me feel
safe or that you love me for who i am.
maybe it's the light inside of your heart.
so although i'll never find the courage
to admit it, *i know that you're the one.*

he looked at me like i was beautiful.
like i was more than the pain
i'd endured. i didn't understand why.
i just knew he made me feel like
i wasn't alone. i've never met someone
like him before. his touch feels like
home and his smile is the purest i've
ever seen. he makes the darkness inside
of my heart want to let go. even when
i'm so lost in fear, i feel sheltered when
he's there. although i've spent my life
running from love, he gives me the
courage to try. i hope he knows he's my
sky, stars, and universe. *i hope he
knows he's everything that makes the
world whole.*

your eyes shined brighter than the
stars that night. i knew that i was in
love. you didn't notice it though.
in my mind, you were there with me.
we danced and laughed until our fear
gave out. we ran to each other and
surrendered control. my heart was
finally at peace. the past seemed like a
faraway dream as i fell into your arms
and suddenly my world was whole
again.
darling, you saved me. you brought me
back to life. *so in my mind, you were in
love with me too.*

you gently held my face in your hands,
your fingertips pressed against my
cheeks. it was in that moment i knew
i was in love with you. i never figured
out the right words to say or how to tell
you. i think the reason you're so special
is because i didn't even have to.
i hope you know i'll never let you go
i hope you know i'll love you until all of
the stars and planets collide.
*i hope you know i'll love you even if
there comes a day when you're no
longer mine.*

"what do you think happens to us after we die?" i asked her. she rolled over to face me, her body lightly trampling the grass.
"i've never really thought about it" she replied. she didn't seem to
consider the depth of my question.
although, it was typical of her to not care for the deeper things.
the sound of crickets filled the air as the stars gave way to her face. we lied on our sides, staring at each other in silence for what seemed like forever. her gaze never seemed to leave me.
"it's just something i've always wondered, you know? i've even come up with a few ideas" i said in an attempt to fill the silence. she gave me a light laugh and rolled her eyes. i know she thinks i'm silly for thinking up these sorts of things. but i can't help it. it's the type of person i am.
"tell me then, darling. i'm curious to see what you've come up with" she smiled. i guess she loves me so she puts up with it.

"maybe it sounds insane, but i think we find peace. i think we're taken to a place where all of our pain and fear no longer have the power to hurt us"
i paused to consider how impossible the words coming out of my mouth sounded. *"can you imagine that?"*
i muttered with a laugh. her hand reached for mine. our fingers gently intertwining.
"i don't have to imagine" she responded with an unusual sense of certainty.
"and why's that?" i asked her, confused on what she meant. she shook her head, her thumb beginning to graze up and down my knuckle. there was something so pure in the way she touched me.
"i don't have to imagine because i already have you"

i love you.
of course, i've never found the courage
to tell you.
i'm not sure i ever will.
but i almost feel as if i don't have to.
because even though i've never said it,
even though i have no proof you feel
the same, i think deep down you know
what we have is more than this.

i think deep down, you know my heart
aches for yours.

and i think deep down, **you love me
too.**

sometimes i get this vision of what my life will look like 10 years from now. it's rather simple. but it makes my heart smile every time i think of it.

i imagine finally finding the courage to be myself. to jump head first into life and love without any fear. i'd meet the girl of my dreams and she'd be the first to ever make me feel at home. we'd laugh about the days when we were so caught up in who the world wanted us to be. she'd drape her arms around my shoulders with a smile. she'd place her head on top of mine and run her fingers through my hair. *and she'd say to me "why would we ever need the world when we hold the entire universe inside our hearts?"*

but in the end, i would go through all of it again. all of the pain and all of the misery. i would climb every mountain, no matter how high. i would live through the nights where i cried so much it felt like i couldn't breathe.
i would watch my loneliness begin to cradle me, surely becoming the only friend i would ever know. and i would once more suffer the pain of watching my heart get broken in two. ***because in the end, it all meant that i would find you.***

i wanted to run to you. i wanted to
jump into your arms and kiss you as
hard as i could, letting go of my fear and
daring to embrace you. darling,
i wanted to scream how much i loved
you.
because you're everything to me.
you're the waves that crash upon the
evening shore. you're every sunrise
after dark. you're the sound of a
thousand lullabies after an eternity lost
in silence. you're the way my heart
aches to let go. you're the calm after
the storm, the rainbow that forms
behind the clouds. you're so beautiful in
all that you do. ***and i just wish you
knew how much i love you***.

about
the
author

Alana Kirby is a poet from Baltimore, Maryland. She's enjoyed writing from the time she was a little girl. But she didn't begin sharing her work online until she was 14 years old. Since doing this, she's gained a massive online following and has inspired hundreds of thousands of people through her words. Helping others through her poetry has instilled a newfound sense of confidence in her passion for writing. She loves being a light to others and finds comfort in knowing others can relate to the emotions and life experiences she's been through.

TikTok: @outsiderpoetpress
Instagram: @outsiderpoetpress

The Words I'll Never Say

The Outsider Poet Press, LLC
6405 Old Harford Road
Baltimore, MD 21214

Cover Design & Layout: Kairos Book Design

ISBN (paperback): 978-1959373155
ISBN (ebook): 978-1959373162